Downpour

Downpour
Ruth Valentine

Smokestack Books
1 Lake Terrace, Grewelthorpe, Ripon HG4 3BU
e-mail: info@smokestack-books.co.uk
www.smokestack-books.co.uk

Copyright 2015,
Ruth Valentine,
all rights reserved.

ISBN 978-0-9931490-8-5

Smokestack Books is
represented by Inpress Ltd

for Ros Finlay

Contents

I
The Message	11
Fiat	12
Girl on Boat	13
Strand	15

II
Death of the Choreographer	19
Downpour	20
The Fiery Furnace	21
After Life	22
Calico	23
Like Snow	24
Scatter-tube	25
The Undertaker's Song	26

III
Extra Care
I	Radiotherapy	29
II	Extra Care	30
III	The North Star	31
IV	Saxon	32

IV
Why I Stole the Keys to the Tower of London	35
Radovan Karadžić at the Hague Tribunal	36
Pietà	38
In Karrada	39
Equinox	40
Shostakovich String Quartet no.15 in E Flat Minor, Opus 144	41

V
The Deliberations of Ereshkigal — 45
I She Studies Psychology — 45
II She Takes Up Music — 46
III She Finds Her Mother — 47
IV She Watches the Riots — 48

VI
The Thaw — 51
Polo-neck — 52
The Sea-Baby — 53
The Baby-Hatch — 57
Driftwood — 58

VII
By the Thames — 61
Long-Term Prognosis — 62

Acknowledgments — 63

I

The Message

In the gutter, the dead fox
remembers grey light through the slatted shed
in the early morning, smell
of dead leaves, chicken bones, nettles.
He lies on his side, very neatly, facing west,
his fur all the colours of seasoned wood,
shadow along his back where the car hit him.
He feels himself stream through a garden fence
into a sunlit bed of yellow poppies

although he's dead. Soon someone will come
from the nearest house, with a shovel. While he can
he pulses out a message to the children
on their way to reception class.
They stop and listen.

Fiat

The snow-light wakes me, swishing across the car.
Drive safely, says my friend on the radio.
I think she has narrow feet, and red-gold hair.
She sits at a desk, the voice
in her earmuffs muttering numbers as she presses
PLAY. Leonard Cohen makes it
colder in here. A black-and-white bramble stares
at its face in the side-mirror. My red-haired friend
is going off-duty: *And wherever you are
have a peaceful night.* I could ring in and tell her
it's sound-proof right back to the main road,
a fox stepped past and I knew it must be her.

The world from this angle
(forty-five degrees, in a ditch) is visibly
curving away, Galileo. My little car
could somersault out into the great nothing
among the static. Imagine me, in orbit
round the earth in a Fiat Uno, studying,
as they top-spin past me, conflict zones and cities,
children in face-paint, women up to their elbows
in last night's dishes, daydreaming, gazing out
at a small blue blob, unlit, and a glass face.

Girl on Boat

mallards busied past her   sequined heads
turning aside   bulrushes   waterboatmen
scribbling on the waterblackboard *crime
seen crime scene*
she rubbed them out with a Coke can
splash   the sun drowned
slowly in reeds   the moon
cut itself into slivers   dropped them in
like bread on the water
bread and punishment
and water   ration the water   the sun came
and went   she was cold   late at night a hand
rose from the current   covered her mouth again

*

today there is no sun
no time like the present
nothing to tell the time

no present
nothing becomes a present

no sound
no shuttered voices
no   no no
today has no past

only the rhythm of the water shaking
the hull of the boat
quietly
like a penance

*

who will splash past
chug past
an outboard motor
a man fishing
a grandfather knowing the inlets
a class of children
five-year-olds shouting at mud
a raft of women
saints with their charts on god

a man   a woman
surfacing through the hard
glass all around her
reproachful
hand in hand

Strand

where there were tall daisies, pepper-scented

where there was dry tamarisk by a stile
and salt grass bending

and sand grew broken rusted sea-defences
from an old war

where draining winter tides scummed up
the fossils of worms

and the wind blew tears   where April
plumtrees were scourged with salt

till the blossom rusted

where the neighbour's lodger died

leaning against the cold of the church wall
with the white dust

of his cure-all salting the bottle beside him
and the waves observed

till after his hearing had poured out   when he cried
voiceless   the seaside town still undisturbed

the seagull voices

II

Death of the Choreographer

The orchestra
halts, in mid-bar. The conductor drops his baton.
At the back, the percussionist
pauses, the cymbals six inches apart.

Already the three wrought-iron tables and chairs
on the stage are looking dusty. The back-projection
turns itself off. The male dancers
lower the women gently. They wait, puzzled.
The consciousness that created them has gone.
They don't exist anywhere any more.
From now on there'll just be the odd moment,
the curtain going up, the *pas de deux*,
that brings them together and straight away discards them.

*

As if another choreographer, at a barre
in an empty rehearsal space, has imagined him.
The dancers look down
from the gods into the set, an avant-garde
white-lit blue-walled room with a low sink
and an empty coffin, him in a hospital gown,
pale blue with daisies, lying on his back,
very still, mouth open,

eyes focussed on elsewhere. If he were the one directing,
any moment now he'd be sitting up and stretching,
swinging his legs round, dropping off the green
hydraulic trolley to an enlivening
spinning *fouetté*. Someone would saunter in,
an undertaker, a mortuary attendant
in rubber boots and white surgical gloves,
take two steps back in amazement and recognition
and lift him high as he rippled out his hands.

Downpour

Rain on a summer evening, not yet dark.
The storm longed for all day has trundled off
to startle some implausible quiet place,
ploughed fields and outbuildings, a shingle beach.
Rain cataracts through foliage, jumps back up
from a flat black roof,
plays downpipes, hoppers, gutters, as if they were
Benjamin Franklin's glass armonica,
liberty as melodious as love.
A woman opens a window, stands aside.
The man she loved for years, years later left,
won't now come back;
she watched his coffin carried in the heat
into the grey stone chapel. No bound flowers,
a few embarrassed speeches, and quite late
that song he once liked.
His son will spread his ashes on the river.
This rain upstream in Marlow or Oxfordshire
reaching Barnes Bridge will swirl and sail him out.

The Fiery Furnace

This woman so short of breath no longer needs it,
like someone who was always short of money
but wins the lottery and moves away
to a big brick house with chauffeur and swimming-pool.

The air that hovered just beyond her shoulder
has burned itself up in the back-room fiery furnace;
like Shadrach, Meshach and Abednego
she has been cast to the flames but not destroyed.

Now finally we see who she really is:
small girl skeetering down a hillside street,
young woman at an island festival,
her baby in her arms, dancing all night.

After Life

First the coffin burns,
then everything you recognised as him,
his hair, the skin of his hands, is vaporised,
two-thousand-degree unanswerable blaze.
The segments of his brain, that once lit up
an MRI scan, now illuminate
the brick walls of this kiln, which is creating
something new from the old form of his being,
since matter cannot destroy itself, but is

reclaimed. When you take the urn in your hands
and feel the weight of him shift, you realise
what you knew as him, what you woke beside at night,
is somewhere else, not as in afterlife,
but as in the cold air in the avenue
of plane-trees outside, the gold leaves darkening
on the grass, the squirrel leaping into winter.

Calico

She has thrown her head back
as if snoring, as if
stargazing, lying star-shaped in a field,
with bird's foot trefoil, speedwell, small bright things
hidden in grass around her, and the small
constellations above her. Her eyes are open,
clouded blue like fragments of bottle-glass
ground rough by the sea, since what she has been seeing
for eighty-seven years has scoured her sight
down to a reflection. We lift her off
the steel tray to her coffin, two of us.
Everything that used to weigh in her is gone,
the tunes she hummed over the washing-up,
the memory in her flesh of the two children
who grew within her and then outside of her
and then away; and her mind's memory,
the swing her father tied to an apple-tree,
the dog at the end of the road, the time her husband
stood at the door, a parcel in his hand.
We wrap the calico round her, tuck it in
over the hands with rose-pink nail-varnish,
the neat stitched place where the mortuary attendant
took out her pacemaker, since she had no further
use for its pace, and mended her again.
All this time she doesn't look at us,
she has other things to contemplate, or else
she's become contemplation. *OK, Maureen,*
we say, and lift the beech lid of the coffin,
lower it over the calico and her face.

Like Snow

Then in that moment everything he's seen
in eighty-five years spills out from his eyes
into the winter air, like snow falling
steadily out of nothing, so the sky
has gone, and the trees are blurred, and the terraced houses –

school, and the days he skived off down the market,
the mountain village in wartime, scavenging,
his wife as he bent towards her by the fire –

all of it rushes out into the space
his consciousness has abandoned, till this man
is him and not-him, the muscle-memory –
chopping wood, carving a joint of meat – disperses

like snowflakes at night, into the neighbourhood
and beyond, so on a hill-farm a woman finds
she can quiet the ewe, ease out the twin lambs.

Scatter-Tube

The dead are out re-configuring the maps
on the Transport for London website. They're joy-riding
with invisible Freedom Passes: the Croydon tram,
the half-hourly bus from nowhere to Wimbledon.
The dead have discovered a new way of getting home
from the mock-Gothic chapel on the South Circular,
in a bluebell-printed cardboard cylinder.
When you open the door you won't know who it is
till he's up on the closed piano, chattering
like he always did: *Call that a supper? Here,
I'll do you an omelette;* but he can't, so there you are
hungry. You go out the back for a cigarette.
The rain's let up, the sunlight is leaching out
like internal bleeding. You open your mouth, the smoke
pleads with the roses that are almost over.
What's left of your calm teeters and falls as ash.

The Undertaker's Song

I am organising the service for the lost:
the Italian men from Glasgow and Clerkenwell
interned in 1940, shipped unescorted
across the Atlantic: for the men who tried
to swim and couldn't, men who were holding on
till they couldn't hold on. This is their funeral.

For eleven hundred and twenty-nine garment workers,
who told the boss there were cracks in the tall building,
were told not to worry and did, but went back up
to their sewing machines and cutting-out machines
and were working in noise and cotton-dust when the building
fell in around them, concrete and cloth and cries.

For the man who dropped out of the landing-gear
of a plane from Angola as it came in to land
at Heathrow. For his hopes and his ignorance,
his family and his courage and the moment
the undercarriage cold gathered him up
into itself and soothed him to a deep

unshakeable sleep. For the pavement where they found him.
Also for this woman present, with tired blue eyes.

III

Extra Care

I Radiotherapy

Don't be afraid. They're taking
a mould of your face,
an anti-death mask for you to slip back on
each morning, when they pour energy through you.

The long drive to the hospital will change,
the bright leaves by the roadside breaking down
to insulation for the snowdrop corms
it's hard to believe in, the beech-mast cracking open.

The cells doing you damage will fall away.
Your face emerging into the spring light
will be yours to live in, your eyes
find skylarks and mottled trout again, your mouth

after its weeks of fasting will long to taste
sea air, the first raspberries, her kiss.

II Extra Care

The dream of the wave
lifting far out. You and I are walking
between the buried breakwaters, each step
sinking us down the shingle. *Look,* I say: tall green water
like the ocean end of a glacier, advancing.

What we're really doing
is buying curtains for the sitting-room
of your new flat, *housing
with extra care,* for when he can come home.
Chrysanthemums, red begonia, light-fittings.
You think he's going to refuse any more treatment.
In the car you light another cigarette,
half-open the window, steer

away from the seafront. What happened next
in the dream I can't tell you, how the beautiful
cliff-face of water broke over my sobbing.

III The North Star

When you locked up the house outside the village
flint walls   red camellia   when you drove down
the dual carriageway between bungalows
to housing-with-care   there were

no lampshades   thick fawn carpets   packing-boxes
no curtains   you had to open all the windows
to let out the heat   room downstairs to recharge
electric buggies
        as if he could motor out
to the North Star   post office   ironmongers

as if he had time enough left to cross the road
at the lights   chug under the tamarisks
past the fish-and-chip shop   feel against his face
wind off the sea   its fine wash-cloth of salt
and see the herring-gulls fall out of light towards him.

IV Saxon

He was afraid of dying in hospital
so he died at home, in the high adjustable
bed, in the step-free flat. For the here and now
you're keeping his ashes next to the photo-box
in the living-room cupboard. You like
still having him here.

No checking the pain-relief, no offering
luke-warm soup, or tea in a feeding-cup;
no changing sheets in the night, and no more waiting
for a word, a grin, one of his corny jokes.
Life with him now is fallow and undemanding.
Most of the time

you try not to remember the afternoons
the two of you went out walking on the Downs
into the wind, the dogs running ahead
and waiting for you to catch up, the chalk emerging
through grass and harebells like an old cleaned bone.
He could be a Saxon,

the warrior buried under the church at Ditchling,
his unknown hopes and travels, his vanished work,
flint and rough sandstone weathering around him.

IV

Why I Stole the Keys to the Tower of London

To smell the blood-stains.
To discuss prison conditions with the ravens.
To lie in a cell writing scallop-shell verses.

To hold the Sovereign's Sceptre in my hand.
To patrol in red-and-gold uniform.
To stand watch over the river for marauders.

To lick the stone,
medieval, Georgian, Tudor.
To bite my tongue.

To mock at treason,
that cuckolded idea.
To instruct the lions.

To bring the Prime Minister and Cabinet
by barge from Westminster to the water-gate.

On Guy Fawkes' Night 2012, a burglar scaled the Front Gate of the Tower and stole a set of keys. He has not been caught.

Radovan Karadžić at the Hague Tribunal

I

He has been an old man with a white beard,
quietly busy in a Belgrade suburb,
neglected prophet: no more uniform,
no more giving orders,

helping as best he could. The foreign lawyers
are Pharisees, Sadducees, with their new-built courtroom.
He refuses to speak to them.
Someone cuts his hair.

> The people that walked in darkness lie in the dark,
> muddled together in pits, in mortuaries,
> laboratories, a bone, a tooth reclaimed,
> given a name-tag. He has written poems,
> he has sat with the distressed
>
> and learned nothing. Let him walk through the forest
> where the women trudged and the fifteen-year-old girl
> hanged herself from a branch.
> Let him stand under the tree.
> Call the tree as witness.

II

He says he *did everything in human power
to avoid the war and reduce the suffering.*
He says whatever exploded in the market
couldn't have been a mortar. He says the bodies
thrown onto trucks were *android mannequins.*
He says he was offered a deal,
should be rewarded.

A shin-bone, a medallion, scrap of hair.
Come to the mortuary: can you identify
this broken arm, the label on this jacket,
this singing voice, this honesty, this skill
with wood or wool, this laughter,
this trust in a future?

III

He is Dragan David Dabič, alliterative
specialist in alternative medicine
and psychology. An understanding man,
he offers the solution to sexual problems
by the use of *Human Quantum Energy*.
He likes his football.

> He's been in prison before, embezzlement,
> and rougher than this.
> On the seventeenth anniversary of what he claims
> never happened, or was exaggerated,
> or someone else's fault, five hundred coffins
> in dark green covers, with a piece of bone
> in each, a buckle, newly identified,

are buried. The trial is taking a long time.
He remembers the head of the Orthodox Church in Greece,
who called him *One of the most prominent
sons of Our Lord Jesus Christ
working for peace.* He prepares his statement.

Pietà

I have said I will never be one of the mourners
in black-and-white photographs, women with helpless cheeks
thin as the starched white cotton of their headscarves,
whose mouths fall open to the eternal shriek
that men make wars, and sons return from slaughter
begging their mothers' blessing. Lamentation
tells the world what it hopes to hear, that rocket-launchers
are toys for Cain and Abel to mark the solstice.
My son was shot crossing the sunlit line
between hunger and dignity. Let his father stand
wailing beside him, willing his eyes to open.
I have left them in slanting light, I have started walking
down through the mountains, past the gun emplacements,
cairns to their own despair, to the guessed-at beach
where waves return from the dead and roar for justice.

In Karrada

from the testimony of Ali, art student, to the journalist Gaith Abdul-Ahad. Baghdad, 20 March 2008

We came, his friends, me and Hassan
and Hadi, and washed him
and put him in a shroud.
He and I would listen to Fairouz
and paint all night.
For six months I didn't talk to anyone.

I saw smoke and chaos and people screaming.
I saw Hassan
running, carrying a child
who'd lost an arm.
The Karrada girls, you know how beautiful,
I saw a girl
who had only one eye.
It is like there is a camera
recording us, and by
its light we see images of death.
I have studied calligraphy for many years.
All I write now are the black mourning signs
and hang them in the street. It is our custom.

Equinox

the clocks went back
clicking against their cogs
unwanted seconds   flashed

so the sun sulked
the clocks

went forward in a line
like boys out of a trench
or women leaving a town
of fallen roofs and tanks

the clocks ran past the hour
evaded its beery breath

just wanted to whirl the sun
dizzily round the earth
rainlight and night to blur
into a shimmered dusk

they wanted to have no time
to consider   to make mistakes

but they couldn't
so then the clocks
wanted it all to stop
to leave things as they were

stone-dust souring the air
bodies beside the road

nothing to get any worse
still they had to keep
pace with the tanks and trains
fear clanging out from a church

magpie on the roof tiles
prodding for life to eat
hopping from house to house.

Shostakovich String Quartet No.15 in E Flat Minor, Opus 144

He has found the place where music
hides when it's frightened, and crouches there beside it,
not for reassurance: to listen to its breathing.
As long as he's there it does carry on breathing,
and sometimes, as if talking in its sleep,
it murmurs a few words in another language,
not its own, and not yet his. The sighing stops,
the air quivers again, until his presence

appears to calm it. He has found the place
he can bear to be now, this burrow in the dark,
the smell of damp topsoil, a little light
from above, at an angle. This is where he is

even when he seems to be in the bar,
at the football ground, or teaching: he's here, watching
at the bedside of music, patiently, in case
it wakes, and turns and smiles at him, recognising.

V

The Deliberations of Ereshkigal

In Sumerian mythology, Ereshkigal is the goddess of the underworld, twice abandoned – exiled at the moment of creation, and left by the god Nergal after seven days and nights of lovemaking.

I   She studies psychology

What we're missing under our ceiling of hacked stone,
while the dead shuffle about and I pretend
to rule them from my lapis and topaz throne,

is weather, puff of warm air across the skin
on the side of your neck, or slate-grey cloud unrolling
upwards from the horizon, wearing thin

till the blue shows through at last; plus all the strange
ways that water finds to sweep down from heaven:
hailstones, crystals, curtains of droplets. Change

of weather, a chance of kindness. If I could have
seasons down here, or thunder, perhaps I'd gaze
less viciously at the dead in our vaulted grave.

II   She takes up music

A temple drum, Tibetan, painted green
and scarlet in segments, with rope loops, to hang
from an arched doorway like a warning gong.
They know about death, she reckons; lifts the curved
beater with the goatskin-padded head –

flump. The sounds drops through the grey air,
flops like a broken egg on the earth floor.
She swings again, willing each note to catch
up with the last and syncopate and keep
the rhythm rebounding through the cobwebbed vaults

till the stone walls hum, the dead leave their catafalques
and march towards her, singing; till the hill
above them throbs like a hive of bees, then cracks,
lets in the sky, that elixir of blue, that smoke,
that melted lapis, and she leads them out –

She drums faster and faster. The thuds collect
around her feet, like droppings, like basalt-dust.

III She finds her mother

There's something missing. In the gap between
creation and exile, before there was any time
for dying to start and the dead to need governing,
there must have been a *mother?*
                              Time to invent one:

big, draped in lots of cloth, and sitting still
(never allowed to leave) in an empty hall
with a pile of blue knitting. Smell of olive-oil soap.

Ereshkigal, under-hill goddess, mountaineers
handhold by slipping foothold, with pitons, ropes,
up the long white skirt to the lap, and looks around.

It's all the same only smaller, the fretful dead
flapping about like flying ants. She grabs
a fold of sleeve to steady herself, and turns

to the face of her made-up mother gazing out
over her head, and smiling. She bounces hard
on what must be a thigh-nerve. Sticks a finger-nail

in a round blue eye. Not a flicker. Leans back against
curved flesh, sucking her thumb. Begins to cry,
experimentally. Nothing. She abseils down,

gathers up firewood from somewhere, stacks it round
the beautiful bare white feet. *You had your chance!*
she shrieks, lighter in hand. The words drizzle back.

IV She watches the riots

When the dead pass
through the seven gates to the air, they'll look like this,
young as they all were once, laughing, athletic,
dancing along the middle of the street
in hundreds, past midnight, petrol can in hand.
When the dead come

at my command
back to the upper world that abandoned them,
how do you think they'll feel? They'll be like these
disappointed kids
grabbing gadgets and trainers, turning over cars,
singing the sound of falling glass. If hope

flourishes somewhere, dares to show itself –
playgrounds, flowers in front gardens – what do you think
the dead can do but torch it and breathe the smoke?

VI

The Thaw

She is the child sealed in the glacier.
A long time ago, high up, beyond the treeline,
where the air scoured clean,
unseen, I dropped her into the azure canyon.
Now she is leaving.
Her hair has grown like ivy, her soap-white hands
are pressing up through the ice, to make the sun
navigate for her. In the villages
I hear the women muttering to her dark
wide-open eyes, I watch the uneasy children
drop poppies across her face; and when the light
opens her glass coffin, I will be there,
clasping my weathered walking-stick, and then
finally I will absolve and bury her.

Polo-Neck

    people sometimes are not
    born   but go on
    acting as if
    they were

    long tendril of
    the passion-fruit vine
    swaying   the place
    in the air between

    the kitchen window   and
    the trellis   where
    it's just withdrawn
    there's always

    shopping to do
    grey polo-neck
    to go with
    grey cord trousers

    the sweater doesn't exist
    but the morning shapes
    hunger around
    its form

    the child aborted
    middle-aged now
    can't keep
    body-warmth in winter

The Sea-Baby

I

scrawny   cries all the time
and the wind flings
hailstones against the window
the waves spit spume
pebbles   green sea-glass   rope
the baby howls

wakes us again
starved sea-wolf
seagull tilting
low over the roof   in warning
the baby vomits

whatever we give it
sheep's milk
stock from bones
grows thinner
and shrieks louder
We know this child

the sea-gods have sent   to stain us
our wealth is gone
seaweed drips from the doorframe
small sea-creatures
crawl from the sand to our kitchen
We have to send

this sea-child back
in the dark
with a slicing moon

then the tide will drain

II

What was it then
we drowned   in a shawl   at midnight
the pale crabs crawled
up from the rock-pools   watching
the seaweed clung
clammy   around our ankles
and the waves

took the baby from us
carefully
tucked it in
under the indigo counterpane
the moon
slid back into the cloudbed
we went to sleep

and woke again to its yowling
It feeds on us
pound by pound of our flesh
it has made us old
the sun comes in at the transom
jeers at us
stooped at our labour
warming sour milk
and rocking

III

The sea-baby
is sticky with seaside rock
candyfloss spun
matting her hair   green cobwebs
the baby stands
alone   on the breakwater

barnacles spiking
pink soles of her feet
smell of seaweed rotting

slides silent   off
into the shrimp pools
oilspills
black sea-urchins

treads sickness
all through the house
watches us bleeding

IV

Little enough to miss us
chrysanthemums
apples will fall and rot
the high-tide wind
shudder the house again
shingle slide from the town
the sea-worms rise
through clay-sand
write their verdict

We lie   calm on our beds
the sea-baby totters
every morning   to observe us
the darkness drops
more often   over our longings
not so long
to wait   till the spring tide
crashes in   claims us

The Baby-Hatch

He spends all day asleep in the Reading Room,
the leather armchair after a hundred years
ponderous, so he dreams
hat-boxes, black leather with silver buckles,
hat-boxes filled with osprey-feathers, combs,
black veils dotted with velvet, yellow roses,
the petals drifting into the silk lining
of the hat-box fat with certainties, christenings.
A hat-box would make a fine travelling-cot,
a way of transporting shame out of the country
and through the mountains, into Switzerland
where they have metal hatches in stone walls
for parents to deposit unwanted children,
like bank accounts never drawn on since the war.

Driftwood

all through the heatwave years
my body was hiding
in the shingle-bank
in the bluebell woods
anywhere

colour and breeze could distract
from a body growing
the sea tossed driftwood
bracken   darkened in rain
I was bewildered

whatever use is a body
of driftwood and bluebell roots
eroded   empty

*

I hid my body
in the pond   under the coot's nest
the heron stood
guard   seven geese
fluttered the water white
my flesh
like water-lily stems
raft to the moorhens

*

ah but my body   if
I'd warmed her   under the sun
she could have woken
day after day   as girls
wake to their fortune

VII

By the Thames

When you're here day after evening, visiting
somebody silent, it helps to look at water.
You take into yourself the shift of water,
its slopping against the stanchions, disturbances
that make the light on the surface fold and vanish,

till by some process maybe light enters him
as he lies on his back. You wonder
what happens in his brain while he's lying still,
if there are colours forming or melodies,
if the ward's clatter and cough still register;

or better, if he's busy at his own
preludes and fugues for a spinet or clavichord,
plaintive, nostalgic, restless, in every key,
major and minor, forty-eight, two for each
day he's been in here, then back to C again.

Long-Term Prognosis

The doctors are saying that there's every chance
there will be a chance, that something new will happen,
you'll be feeling something you're not feeling today,
that morning will come and you'll be here to see it

or be here but not see it. The doctors are saying
they are doing their best. They're saying they understand
more than they don't understand, that your condition
is stable, given the trembling of the stars

and the circulation of breath. All the good doctors
are wringing their hands or perhaps washing their hands
or rubbing hand-hygiene gel over their hands,
along their fingers and across the webbing

between thumb and first finger, with which they point
to charts and scans and the overall direction,
which is towards their own death and your death,
the death of the planet and the death of hope

which of all things they aim to keep alive.
When you leave your white hospital bed to someone
with more need of their attention, hope will climb
up the steep side of the undersheet, lie back

relieved, against several pillows, and, docile, watch
the thermometer homing in on its open mouth.
Hope will be sitting cheerfully up in bed,
surrounded by cards and x-rays and relatives,

while you are wheeled along the corridors,
no longer in pain, a sheet over your face.

Acknowledgments

Thanks are due to the editors of the following publications where some of these poems were first published –*Acumen, The Bow-Wow Shop, Critical Quarterly, The Frogmore Papers, London Grip, Poetry London* and *Poetry Salzburg Review*. 'Calico' won second prize in the 2015 Troubadour poetry competition.